LOGICIAN OF THE WIND

Also by Lee Slonimsky

•

POETRY

Pythagoras in Love (an Orchises Book)
Talk Between Leaf and Skin
Money and Light

•

FICTION (as Lee Carroll, with Carol Goodman)

Black Swan Rising
The Watchtower

LOGICIAN OF THE WIND

Lee Slonimsky

•

Orchises

Washington

2012

Library of Congress Cataloging Publication Data

Slonimsky, Lee.
Logician of the wind / Lee Slonimsky.
p. cm.
ISBN 978-1-932535-27-3 (alk. paper)
I. Title.
PS3619.L67L64 2012
811'.6--dc23

2011028464

ACKNOWLEDGMENTS

The following people have been supportive of my poetry the past few years during which most of the poems in this collection were written:

Peter Bricklebank, the late Roger Bobley, Mrs. Lyn Chase, Elizabeth Coleman (intense appreciation for her brilliant translation of *Pythagoras in Love* into French), Rhina P. Espaillat, Daniel Fernandez, Jack Foley, my wife Carol Goodman (special thanks for her insightful ordering of poems!), Marcia Golub, Rachel Hadas, Katherine Hastings, Daniel Hoffman, Helen Handley Houghton, my mother Elinor Kay, X. J. Kennedy, Roger Lathbury, Kevin Pilkington, Supritha Rajan, Mike Robbins, Michael Salcman, Joe Salemi, Nancy Mellichamp Savo, my daughter Nora Slonimsky (special thanks for her astute ordering of poems!), A. E. Stallings, Karen Swenson, Maggie Vicknair and Pui Ying Wong. I wish to acknowledge the influence and inspiration of the following locales: Inwood Hill and Van Cortlandt Parks in New York City, greenest walk in Woodstock, NY, and Santa Fé, NM.

Many thanks to the editors of the journals in which a number of these poems first appeared, sometimes in different form or under another title: *Atlanta Review, Blueline, The Carolina Quarterly, The Classical Outlook, Classical World*, the novels *The Drowning Tree* and *The Night Villa* by Carol Goodman (Ballantine Books, 2003 and 2008), *Home Planet News*, the novel *Mating Rituals* by Lauren Lipton (Grand Central Publishing, 2009), *Measure, Manhattan Poetry Review, The New York Times, North Dakota Quarterly, Per Contra, River Oak Review, Sulphur River Literary Review Press, 32 Poems*, and *Trinacria*.

"Discovery" was the 2008 centennial poem of the Classical Association of the Atlantic States. "Professor (Emeritus)" won first prize in the 2007 Greenburgh, NY poetry contest.

Orchises Press • P. O. Box 320533 • Alexandria, VA • 22320-4533

For my brother JOEL, *sports fan extraordinaire*

CONTENTS

ONE

Two

ONE

HORSE

A billion years ago or more, we split:
one branch of DNA became the plants,
the other, animals. Amœbae, ants,
eventually us with all our wars and wit.
And so this gnarled old oak should not surprise,
its massive knot a perfect horse's head —
such natural craftsmanship — both branches wed
in a quaint sculpture, yet exact and wise
in summary of science. But the snort
you hear quite suddenly, flapping of tails,
unnerve; then stomp of hooves truly startles;
it conjures wind and gallop, courage, heart.
Whatever's in there yearns so to be free,
you want to liberate it from this tree.

DNA AT DAWN

Soft mist that wreathes an indistinct shape glows
at early light, then sparkles in a breeze
the river conjures from this summer haze
and first chill hint of autumn. Water knows
our history better than any book:
its cycles lush with wax, then sparse with wane,
but ceaseless flow, a sliver of time's reign
that overwhelms all flim and flutter. Take

a moment to behold this shape, which gleams,
clearer now in brighter air: storm-snapped tree,
one branch resembling bird that wants to flee
a wooden home of gnarl and stump. Almost a dream
of where we come from, possibly that tree
whose cells once took a walk. And made us free.

THE MENORAH TREE

Its curving branches: candelabra-like.

Remarkable, how treeshape is an art
of evolution. Maybe there's an Ark
in nearby grove of leafy oaks. Let's look.

But though we walk the rest of that slow day,
Menorah Tree is singular.

                 Deny
a deity — conversely, kneel and pray —
the tree is there both ways, with orange sky
an inkling of the sun's eternal flame,
or almost so. Sun dies well down the road
but much to bask in, if for now. My name
and those of forebears and descendents fades
yet something's in the coldest wind that lasts,
that sources tangled roots in the deep past.

BEECH

A pair of branches strikes a pose of prayer,
or maybe it's beseeching the March wind
to mellow just a little, tint the air
with tiny hint of balm, of coming spring.

The branches at midtrunk emerge like twins,
near-parallel, suggesting some intent;
as if bark has nerve endings from a brain
somehow embedded in the crown aloft.

Historians of DNA say
that rooted beings and we mobile cousins split
about a billion years ago. Perhaps
this beech is feeling some late day regret
as birds fly grandly in the orange haze,
and it can only stand there chilled; await
the earth's rotation toward a warmer fate.

LATE LIGHT

This tree has learned much math, its shape suggests,
perhaps beginning when it was a seed,
and so it loves the perpendicular,
the slant and horizontal, more than air
or life itself. And it will count its leaves
each April and October; then it rests
in winter's starkness, roots savants of curve,
longing for summer's seethe
each time the north wind swerves.

It cannot speak in the Academy
of this theorem or that; its knowledge is
deep in its cells, a bark-geometry
that slants from wind, that sometimes slowly sways,
as if to show a ratio of height
to calm-then-gust, of branches to late light.

PERSPECTIVE

I am the humblest pebble you might kick,
or skip across the pond to show your strength,
but I was born a billion years ago,
and my distinguished lineage will show
the most modest deserve a second look,
while grandiosity's often a feint
by emptiness to gain respect. I glow

with an incandescent reverie of *then*:
how lava's fire so polished me that I
stay warm in January even now;
(the miracle of memory allows
a kind of second eye, oval like me),

but still there is a sadness to the *then:*

I'm better off enjoying present spin,
this instant reckless stage of being flung.

CHARLEMAGNE

So capillary-like, twigs merge with air;
slow wind massages wood like blood does flesh;
all union is the size of molecules,
as is the earth's most vital history:
amino acids, living cells combined
in spheres that make bright leaves gargantuan,
a branch or two almost a universe,
and one black worm the Charlemagne of mud.

And what does size make us, so self-content,
observing all this richness from a bench?
Not much, it seems, for time's a bigger size
than space or wealth or all the stars that burn,
one in which we're less stable than the wind,
minute as motes a fall wind loves to spin.

The worm does not give up. Time and again,
it wriggles past pebbles and goes on home.

COLLEAGUES

Methodical, this ant's approach to light
explored beneath a moss-kissed shard of log —
he traces a bright trapezoid of bog
rays color yellow — lover of all lines,
the way shadow and gleam divide meek sight
into blur and pure shape. Antcrawl defines
a rudimentary geometry,
a lecture in minute trajectory
that startles and excites Pythagoras —
who longs to share ideas, and casts about
for common language — notes his abacus
and places it so his colleague can crawl,
counting the dewslick beads. A sacred route,
revealing truth to him: they share a soul.

MANY LIVES LATER: TRIANGULATION

On a recent walk through Van Cortlandt Park, I encountered a red-tailed hawk. As I walked across a field bordering some woods the bird circled over my head, then perched on an oak branch high above.

I gazed up at her, and she returned my stare for a few minutes. Then she swooped down directly at me, and leveled off to a glide no more than twenty feet over my head. For an instant, I thought I'd have to protect myself. It gradually dawned on me that the hawk had regarded me as an intruder.

Leaving the park, I approached my car and observed the simultaneous arrival of two cars at one parking space. The first car had driven up while the other made a broken u-turn, targeting the same space. Both drivers honked several times and glared at each other. Neither seemed willing to move.

I drove away, reflecting on a common trait displayed by two otherwise very different-looking species.

THE SQUARE ROOT OF GLIDE

Triangulate these platinum hot rays
descending from their hazy shroud of cloud
to glisten on long dewdrenched leaves,

                                    with pond's
green shimmer, and hypotenuse of breeze,

to calculate gray hawk's square root of glide,
of azure soar, trajectory beyond
far sunstreaked hill, returning in ellipse
of wing-etched, taloned ease.

                            P can't decide
what's more impressive, flight's geometry
or what her view must be from cloud ribbed perch;
he longs to gaze from heights. . . a sudden lurch,
then surge aloft, as wings begin to grow

upon his back.

This world of seethe and turmoil slips away,
replaced by slow ascent and glide toward sun.

FUSION

Trees are the scholars of biology —
no doctorates, or fellowships, or robes —
but intuition, perspicacity.

Yet earth is riddled with so many woes
and trials, potential deep calamities,
like asteroid collisions, sun's demise;
no refuge either in noon's sunny breeze
or twinkling stars to come: those are mere lies
of sparkle, shimmer. Fusion is their core,
that same which threatens our farewell in war.

But here we'll laze our heads back in the grass,
and let trees lecture us on sway and balm;
our *now* so swiftly merges with the past,
while leafy scholars talk of love and calm.

THE LANGUAGE OF TREES

You told me trees could speak
and the only reason one heard
silence in the forest
was that they all had been born
knowing different languages.

That night I went in the woods
to bury dictionaries under roots,
so many books in so many tongues
as to insure speech.

And now, this very moment,
the forest seems alive
with whispers and murmurs and rumblings of sound
wind-rushed into my ears.

I do not speak any language
that crosses the silence around me,
but how soothing instead to know

that the yearning and grasping embodied
in trees' convoluted and startling shapes
is finally being fulfilled
in their wind shouts to each other.

Yet we who both speak English
and have since we were born
are moving ever farther apart
even as branch tips touch.

SEASIDE BENCH, SORRENTO

When Wilhelmina F. Jashemski found
Vesuvius had outlined some ghost-roots
of trees beneath the lava-sheeted ground —
empty spaces traced with pebbles — missing truths
of leaf and bark, species, were brought to light.
Her plaster casts could resurrect the dead,
at least as sculpture, art.

                    And now the flight
of sea hawks hints at pterodactyl blood
while ancient sunlight shimmers on the bay,
and our thoughts turn to love, which if it lasts
a year will flirt with immortality.

Vesuvius has nothing new to say,
haze-shrouded, calm. This all goes by so fast.

There's more than one kind of catastrophe.

FLIRTING

Philosophers of veer, savants of glide,
these swallows fly with passion too sometimes:
as if they're tracing love along the lines
of sunset, shadow-dappled by red leaves
of maples, elms that crowd the mountainside.

Much flirting suddenly, their quick sweet weaves
of swoop and flutter, mating rituals
P took part in himself so long ago —
reluctantly — Elena would soon flee
his self-absorption to be royally wed
in Sicily. Later, with his wife who fills
his heart with longing now, in slow exile.

                                                   Slow too
this single bird's trajectory:

P hates when love ends in catastrophe.

DISCOVERY

Without its classicists the world is bare,
utilitarian and dry as bone;
machinery rules even softest air
and dust obscures the thought of Greece and Rome.
But just as Keats once found exotic seas
in Chapman's Homer, so discovery
of Ovid and Catullus, Sophocles,
came to our youth in this past century,
thanks to the efforts of all those who teach,
and write, and love a vanished ancient realm
which otherwise would be beyond all reach:
they save us from a tide that overwhelms,
and give to us our crucial legacy —
the past — bright glimmer of eternity.

Tiberius's Villa

With stones this ancient one could write a poem,
if only cruelty were beauty too;
what inspiration, rocks necklaced with foam
where used-up lovers met their mangled doom.
But actually it's stark — quite hideous —
to picture them hung from a precipice,
Tiberius's victims, innocent,
eyes blinking back bright dawn — then down they went.

The sea remembers well what time denies,
in supple surge and shimmer, sudden crash,
and gulls recall it too, in glides and dives;
a scarlet sunset tints to blood their splash,
a falcon's soar, the late day breeze, some clouds
that streak twilight. Now how the darkness broods.

Jean Robin, Botanist to the French King (1602)

Voluptuous, these trees that bask in May;
just weeks ago their nudity was stark;
twigs, branches spearing pale late winter air
as if defending pulse from freeze. The stare,
caresses that he gives an oak display
an ardor only half human. Its bark
excites him so, and oh those supple roots!
He lusts for lush, this royal botanist
who sublimates his urges in clenched fists,
whose blushes mirror pink-rosed dawn. There stirs
so deep within his halfgreen trembling heart,
a different ancestry: it lulls. Then roars.
It's sapveined, soaked with ancient chlorophyl,
and speaks to him of time immemorial.

WIDOW IN THE WOODS

A hundred years or more, she's bent her crown
in storm, in sun, in moonsplashed midnight breeze,
surviving all the random vagaries
of this harsh world. A dense-twigged veil drifts down
from crown, along her trunk — mourning slow wood —
that rustles, tattered, in a hint of wind
this January dusk, cloudy, purpling
the ground with sudden shadows.

                               How she broods —
you speculate — on dark surprise and loss,
alone these many years, despondent, bent,
her bolt-cracked mate transformed to splinters, moss.
Though not alone, you feel the sadness of
a twilight breeze. There's never enough love;
the widow nods to you. Her branches moan.

CONSOLATION

No logic to such mangle can be found:
storm-shatter has cleaved oaks to blasted wrecks,
gnarled thirds in manic sprawls, from brambled crowns
to splintered trunks. Lightning's bolt-craft astounds,
creating three from one. P on a rock
is contemplating suddenness of split,
collapse, muck merge, the random slash of fate.

A hundred years to grow, ten seconds down.

It gnaws at his world view, this tangled doom
that could be his as well. He's not immune
to quick vicissitude; an intellect
serves to investigate, not to protect.
But P finds some small solace, finally:
like triangles, lightning can think in threes.

INNOCENT

I've been an atom deep inside an oak
for near a century now. But this wind
is threatening, the severing kind, and. . .
crack! The trunk is split; I'm free to look
at lightning, red clouds, summer's thrash at dusk.

At peace, I bask in weather, gazing up
even when rain begins to fall. "Relax,"
I tell my gnat-electrons, "take your loops
as slow as moonrise — we can sail the air
now that our tree is halved, and glide to Rome
or Santa Fe or Mars; a star's not far —

or we can stay and call this gnarled stump home."

An oak's a cell of beauty; who could have known
its sad limits? I love our freedom so.

MANY LIVES LATER: FREEDOM

I was taking a walk through Van Cortlandt Park when I encountered a rabbit that I recognized from some white markings. I had not seen it in several months. During its absence I had feared the worst, perhaps from a winter storm or an encounter with a red-tailed hawk, so I spied it with relief.

A few minutes later I observed a police car drive into the park, all the way to the edge of woods a few yards in front of me. Two officers got out and one removed a blue carrying case with air holes from the trunk.

"I thought we were going to release it further inside the park," one officer said to the other.

"But it's only a rabbit," her partner replied. "And besides, it likes people. Remember, it's been a pet."

I took a moment to reflect on the converging circumstances of two rabbits, one prevailing over the uncertainties of life in the wild, the other about to taste freedom for the first time.

SWEETNESS

I was an atom in a girder, Yankee Stadium,
from Ruth to Mantle till girders were removed
for more sightlines, and all us atoms moved
to south New Jersey, to the *crash-then-hum*
of mall construction. Nowadays I sit,
in iron near aluminum, and watch
the shoppers as they shake their heads then flit
from red shoes to dark green. I'm in a latch
attached to a skylight so I can root
as well for cumulus against cirrus — not Joe
nor Lou nor Yogi, Roger Maris, Mo —
but weather is a kind of team sport still. Sweet,
those days when blue sky wins its victories
against small hints of gray, a chilly breeze.

EXCURSION

Slow stream delights in shaping rough to round,
for which it's practiced for eons; it scoops
bright spheres from jagged stones, as swallow loops
tie summer air in bows. Stream-shimmer smoothes
erratica of grain and crack to loss
as if effacing stress — without a sound —
and with a robust deep delight that moves
us to reflect on simplifying. . . peace.

But water has the centuries to grow,
decide on change, ripple, cavort with moods;
we've barely stolen this one hour to brood
on overwork and emptiness, our slow
but certain drain-away. Windy leaf flits
from light toward shadow like it has a mind
and maybe that's the central point of it:
to merge with flow, to move outside of time.

SHIPWRECK REEF

These birds that migrate seven thousand miles:
they have the urge to travel. What a leaf,
October-yellowed, spiraling down, must feel
if oh so briefly. Ant makes use of guile
to circumvent a pebble, wanders too,
and so do you. You've told your boss "I'm through,"
dartboarded destination — Shipwreck Reef —
and now you laze on shore without belief
in any future. Plans and headaches flew
in one winged moment out the window; jazz
might be an interest, or photography
but somehow you don't know. The ocean smiles
back at you like some cool prosperity:
you sip your drink, enjoying kick and fizz,
quite low on cash but wondering if wander
will turn out to be worth its weight in plunder.

TWO

RIVALS

The beauty of a concentricity
of pebbled ripples is obedience
to laws of shape and speed, a fluid Pi
suggesting stone and water's sentience,
number ruling shimmer.
                               What aesthetics in
the please of patterns, black fly loops
and snakeslick undulations, mirror's tricks
played by a branch-etched pond. A swallow's swoops.

How humbling, though, that rays' trajectories
are so well plotted, that bullfrogs can count
to five and six in — thrum, response — a breeze,
perform equations abacus cannot.

His mind's no greater than this floating bee's,
mere sliver of the sun's. Bright leaf agrees.

Rainy Day

This morning, through the slosh and quag of muck,
the rain torrents, through squish and splash of step,
I heard the croak,

a mud-mirrored bull twang from glossy green
owner of windstrewn pond. Protest
against weather's denial of lust,
perhaps, but then again
the joy of boom
has resonated since late trilobite.

His answer was just to himself,
a low dark moan.

Nothing like a rainy day
to feel so quite alone.

SWALLOW

P longs to measure concentricity,
a quality of pebbled ripples, rings
of oaks, the ovals hawks etch with their wings
as they drift lower, slower while scanning
the woods for scurry, flit.
                              Geometry
instructs in area, but not in pace
or pulse or ratio of speed to space,
sublime pond artistry that leaves no trace,
designs in air that wind and clouds efface. . .

but solid stump endures. The history
of wood is written round, its author Pi;
one theme's that theorems prove the here and why
of every leaf and gnarl. A second text on loops
may find papyrus in a swallow's swoops.

CIRCLES

So many times, this duck has dipped her bill
and circled ripples from it to the shore,
while overhead two hawks in lofty soar
have intertwined ellipses, flown until
the sun has circled down behind the hill
that shadows this green pond. Yet even more
concentric circles spread; now ducks are four
relentless math-aquarians who still
nod on through dusk, each steadfast bobbing head
amazing P till after dark. He'll stay
to watch this pattern, how these birds obey
geometry, how shape and water wed.
The primacy of circles fills this pond,
as well as ruling all the world beyond.

Uncertain

Tangle, bramble, wind-demented sprawl;
the woods in wake of storm praise chaos well.
Observed from high above, from flowered hill,
such wrack and ruin's a fine logician's hell:
bolt-splintered trunks and muck-smeared branches scrawl
a litany of why not to believe;
and nothing, not the symmetry of leaves,
nor roundness of the sun, nor rays' straight lines
persuade P of a meaningful design.
But he takes pleasure anyway, this dawn,
in minute logic's spell. Philosophy
from perfect spacing in a warbler's notes,
the gentle arcs on which a plump bee floats
from purple to pale pink. Then there's the sea
beyond the forest, glimmering slow waves
obeying math. The diamond foam believes.

GEOMETER

Cloud-slit sunslant is mirrored in this pond,
a sorcery of opposed triangles
bisected by the raysplashed flight of gulls,

suggesting a geometry P can't
quite fathom, theorems just beyond
his acumen.
                A trigonometry
of water, light and symmetry intrigues
when organizing space, but he's uncertain of
its theorems;
              concentrates
instead on clashing vectors (wren and breeze),
air's angles under flash of fluttering wings,
the secret to aloft.

            He'll calculate
a formula for soar until fatigued,
then dream of what pond theorems just might be.

WIND

This hilltop pond's a well-schooled sorcerer
in conjuring of fir trees, wispy clouds
from green and crystal depths. Pythagoras,
distressed by senses' imperfection, broods
on how closely the trees below reflect
their cousins spearing sky. And now, were he
to put his hand in water, it would merge
with branches in a shimmering mirage.

He wonders if the eyes' bold lies, matter's,
(misleading as slow morning's trickery
of light and water), are meant to instruct
him in raw solitude. Then sudden chill:
one fleeting breeze makes mirror into blur.

Beyond the intellect, there's nature's will.

SPEAR

The forest that's reflected in this pond
looks just as real as wispy clouds or sky,
suggesting that the senses are a lie
and any truth or constant is beyond
a world always in flux.
                     Feel this leaf
in early June, shimmering with cold dew
at dawn. Green spear. No question of belief
in its solidity, but right below
hand's grasp of it in water shakes the eye.

Perhaps perfection's in asymmetry
of faith and doubt, chaos and abacus:

as wind may blur a hawk's hypotenuse
of sunglazed soar; cloud-shadows smear pond's woods;
disorder be one whole. Or so P broods.

GEOMETRY AND THE MOON

(according to Iamblichus, Midas was the name of one of Pythagoras's students)

"Geometry's Egyptian," Midas claims,
one afternoon while shadows measure wind
by fluttering each time new gusts begin,
until the air turns still, and sunset frames
horizon's subtle curve with its gold flames.
"What better way to keep the rain within
their growing fields, the earth's green flowered skin,
than seeding where math's fertile arrow aims?"

Pythagoras must sigh; he has to doubt
the authenticity of looselipped tales:
"Geometry arises from all shapes,
from essences no earthly form escapes.
This late day sky's what theorems are about;
then starsplit seas the moon so smoothly sails."

MATH OF MUSIC

An abacus of deep woods' dappled leaves
is useful to the math of mockingbirds,
an easy way of counting harmonies
to multiply by noon, divide by slant
of late day rays. To plot geometries
of subtly shifting shadows, crimson tints
they can convert to integers of lilt,
and pass along through song, lacking the words
to teach their young.
                    Their math-notes must suffice
for language, culture, solace of belief
in something more than matter. As mere leaves
aspire toward the high (spear sudden breezes
in quest for light), so certainly these birds
demand a patterned world, a thought-rich peace.

MANY LIVES LATER: THE OPERA SINGER

I was walking along the Putnam Trail of Van Cortlandt Park, which has isolated sections that can make any stroller nervous. As I approached the Henry Hudson Parkway, which crosses above the trail, I spied a shabbily dressed man standing under the arched overpass, glancing furtively at me.

As I got closer, he walked away from me toward the obscurity of dense underbrush nearby. I found myself accelerating my pace as I strolled past him, and I could feel tension in the back of my neck. I glanced back more than once to see if he was following me. He wasn't.

Then I heard the most mellifluous baritone imaginable, coming from where the man had concealed himself, a baritone that floated through the wind-rippled greenery as if an opera had begun. I recognized the Italian language, but not the opera.

His shyness, it turned out, was that of the artist in need of privacy, his shabbiness an indication that the job market must not be thriving for opera singers, either.

TRANSUBSTANTIATION

Achieving perfect stillness daunts the air
but is routine to this old massive tree,
a slab of stone, an ant's repose, the sear
of sun itself at summer noon. P feels free
when meditating, more than in his quest
for calculation's latest truth. The slow
reflective thought of leaves he much admires,
emancipation from quenchless desires
and all the sharp regrets fate will bestow.

Savants who can command rivers to rest,
well-rumored to the east, newly inspire,
and now as air brisks up P leans through breeze
and dreams himself a rock, a prince of ease
who knows no obstacles, not even flames.
Such transubstantiation is fine balm
for sear of toss and fro. In noon's storm, calm.

METAPONTUM

This yellow leaf's the only calendar
the summer needs to mark a tilt toward fall;

it floats as lazily as light at noon,
slow-spiral-down in surest hint of

                               soon,
a north wind chills late summer's shimmer, sear,
then leaves obey oblivion's strict rules,
their color-drift and crackle marking time
until first frost makes dawn a dazzling gleam.

For now leafspin evokes serenity,
the patience of the earth with simmering breeze;

there were slight seasons in south Italy,
but weather here will make him pause. Geometry
is good enough in its own way but wind
tells everything when to begin or end.

EXILE, NOVEMBER

This brittle weather breaks in snow's deluge
soon enough. The sky right now so frail,
P broods on eggshell clouds and pale gray winds
as if he's not sure where stormspeech begins
and quiet ends. But gliding swallows sail
as though the air is balm; last foliage
suggests a hint of fire inside ice.
P lets the hope of opposites entice
despite slow drear and wan, until the thought
of Croton's endless summer makes him weep.

The present never can be quite as sweet
as memory, or oscillating hope.

Some consolation comes in swallows' swoops,
and how they mime his math in windkissed loops.

MANY LIVES LATER: RAIN, BIRDS

February wanes
and each raindrop's a geometer
etching perfect ripple-circles
in the puddles at your feet.

Only two weeks ago,
raindrops would have been snowflakes.

Amazing how water knows
its Euclid and Pythagoras —
despite lack of an abacus —
its radii, diameters, and Pi,
enough so concentricity
of ripples can instruct
a dragonfly, a wren
or even circling clouds
in a slowly brightening sky.

Just like the earth's rich seasons know
dividing wind by four,
from balm to blow to howl to fair,
mathematics in the air
like physics in the stars,
or hummingbirds who've gone to school
to learn the sum of wingbeats
to hover like the sun.

And birds who migrate mightily,
seven or eight, ten thousand miles
have studied with the wisest mountains —
their glistening domecaps of snow
like scholars' caps of long ago
showing what they know —
to find their eggs where science's
cold instruments could not.

That's scholarship beyond the wind,
or libraries, human genomes,
and yet birds can be sliced for lunch
as surely as a cold wind blows.

PROTEGÉ

The way this ancient trunk's been sundered, split
in semicircle halves, moss-streaked and long,
suggests lightning that knew geometry
and practiced it in action. Even leaves
will get one chance in autumn, spiraling down
to show knowledge of circles. While P's bound,
in exile, to stark anonymity,
an audience of silence, stones and breeze.

Except one sunny morning: now he's found
a gold-bird protegé, the sun made flesh.
Each object that he touches, this bird counts:
a twig is two trills, bark three, water four,
beyond all random possibilities.
Alone no more, P basks in chirps that reassure.

Return from Exile

Exhilarated on his long-walked path,
Pythagoras, rejuvenated, basks
in lush sunlight and for a moment asks
why numbers matter, if the height and width
of triangles explains this awe, this *Is*
of branchery, smooth stones, the love of blue
for sky and water. How the wind, once true
to winter, now's the tickle of soft breeze.

Exiled so long, he'll soon be gone, but still
the shimmer of the pond slows sullen time
almost to sweet oblivion. His will
can make a lot of what is left. Sublime,
the way age can lift attitude, rouse hope:

he gazes at some swallows' perfect loops.

Professor (Emeritus)

The most precocious of his students are
these hummingbirds, geometers of flit,
savants of hover, scholars of June air:

their formulae can stabilize a breeze,
triangulate sunlight and gnarls on trees,
calculate a worm's trajectory
as it divides muck in its sluggish surge.

Pythagoras, impressed, cannot compete
with how they gauge swift raysplashed angles, merge
feathered scholarship with dart and dance.

                                        He tries

to count their wingbeats on his abacus,
divide into warm wind, except his eyes
have trouble following the emerald blur,
which makes more difficult a measurement
of ratio of glide to how wings whir.

LIMITS

P seeks a way to capture ecstacy
in numbers; theorems that might quantify
the start of love, or how a scarlet sky
perfects a poignant mood. But two or three
or nine fall short when used to try to prove
that rapture comes by grace of formula,
elation's wings align with logic's soar,
or the right count inspires blood to love.

Age gives perspective; he must acquiesce
in autumn's haze, slow ripples on a pond
when chill breeze stirs; in limits of pure math
for making sense of life. No point to wrath,
regret or slow despair, each just a mood
in rhythm with the wind: no more, no less.

MEDITATION

The only way to soothe all seethe is math —
to organize this flit and flash — a dawn
of sunstreaked pond and blackbird swoops belongs
to number just as much as swirl.
                                 P's path
divides a quotient of the queerly gnarled,
the jagged, looped and smeared. He'll multiply
damp leaves by shimmer, slant, and thus derive
a formula for gloss of dew; he'll turn
June's sprawl and burst into green symmetries.

And yet the unexpected will allure:
here a gash, there a tangle, larks
wind interrupts, gusts splashing notes like leaves
a coming rain will drench.

                              Without surprise,
he does wonder if gauge keeps him alive.

REFUSAL

This world of wounds may need a savior now,
but he won't be the one — no taste for crowds,
or hollow shimmer of sudden acclaim —
he doesn't care how many know his name.

Last night's beseechers gone, he sits and broods —
let self-importants lead — he must follow
dawn sun up slow trajectory, oak trees
whose pacifism guides a mild wet breeze,
an ant, a beetle, worm, swooping swallows,
and all the world that's not at war. Ignore
the dazzle of illusory esteem.

Greek wounds could heal but he thinks, at the core,
humanity's violent. As flowers sway,
better to just observe a slow new day.

ANOTHER WARBLER

"The secret was in stillness, not contortion."
Marcia Golub, *Tale of the Forgotten Woman*

Longevity wears lightly on this oak,

gnarled once or twice for sure, but morning sun
dresses it in a sleek vivacity

Pythagoras envies. His muscles ache
so early on his walk now, age has won
a skirmish that unnerves. Geometry
and abacus sustain, and on he'll fight
for as long as he can, but more subdued
than in his youth, or just last week.

                    A breeze
massages as he rests, as does slow light;
he hopes fatigue is just a mood
and doggedly pushes on. These ancient trees
still cloak themselves in shimmer. Flash of wings,
and he's ready to count; a warbler sings.

Rehearsal

P's nap this afternoon is practice for
a longer one; he slumbers in a grove —
his bed thick grass — oblivious to soar
of hawk-geometers, to how clouds move.
Instead he drowses while he calculates
the sluggishness of bees in summer's seethe,
a pensiveness in how black spiders weave
amidst bronze shimmer. All life feels the heat,
he guesses, from the way leaves curl and droop. . .
And soon enough he sleeps; his atoms slow,
rehearsing for eternity. They'll go
into the vast primordial soon enough;
meanwhile he dreams of dragonflies, their loops,
and how their summer love's a perfect truth.

SWAY

This *red leaf love* defies mortality
for just an instant.

Windstrewn October, yet it warms my blood
as if I were still human.

           Now a tree
for centuries, with slow days fine to brood
on this and that, an ant's bark-climb, a wren
who's built her nest amidst my lush and gleam
(fast scarleting),

           I find fall's tinted swoon
warms lustrous air, and cloaks me to my roots. . .

I've had five lives all told, none what they seem —
as gnat, bat, toad, Pythagoras, all truths
and yet mere visages, clay, blur of dreams —
a move from one to none, then back again.

I seek serenity, or love; a friend
to sway with me in wind and cheat the end.